IN SEARCH OF
JESUS OF NAZARETH
AND
HIS ORIGINAL TEACHING

by

Paul A. Weekes

DORRANCE
PUBLISHING CO
EST. 1920
PITTSBURGH, PENNSYLVANIA 15238

Dorrance Publishing Co
585 Alpha Drive
Pittsburgh, PA 15238
Visit our website at www.dorrancebookstore.com

ISBN: 978-1-6470-2323-2
eISBN: 978-1-6470-2792-6

To: Maria G. Martin Horta

"The light of my life"

Preface

This book chronicles my personal research and analysis in a quest to understand the historical Jesus and His original teachings. I do not ask anyone to accept my conclusions, but rather to use the book as a guide in clarifying their own faith and belief.

Paul Weekes

Contents

INTRODUCTION

All of the great religious leaders/teachers (Abraham, Moses, Jesus, Muhammad, Buddha, Confucius, etc.) were involved in responding to a special spiritual calling/communication with a universal power that most people refer to as "God." There are many powerful influences that control the physical universe, including: gravitational, centrifugal, magnetic, electrical, atomic, and nuclear forces. Similarly, there are forces contained within every human being on Earth that influence the direction and quality of that individual's life. Among these forces are self-preservation, ego, and what I will call the "life force" for good. All of the luminaries above and many more, including Aristotle, Socrates, Da Vinci, Newton, Bach, Lincoln, Gandhi, Einstein, Martin Luther King, and Mother Teresa, were clearly operating on a heightened level of life force. This life force is also known as: the soul, the Divine Spirit, the conscience, morality, spirituality, or what the Dalai Lama identified as "ethical compassion" in a May 5, 2009, speech at MIT. He also indicated, "There's potential to increase that internal force, just as knowledge can be increased by education." Jesus of Nazareth declared that the same internal force that drove him was in every individual, and he called it "the Kingdom of God."

Background

I grew up in Central New York State during the 1940s and 50s. My father passed away when I was seven, and my mother believed that I would benefit from religious instruction. So, I attended the required classes and was confirmed as a member of the Episcopal Church. While I understand that it has become much more liberal, at that time, the Episcopal Church was "Catholic-Light." The only difference was that divorce was allowed, and the services were not conducted in Latin. Even at that early age, I was math- and science-oriented and had a great deal of difficulty buying into the religious dogma of a flat world, Jonah and the Whale, the Sun revolving around the Earth, walking on water, etc. My takeaway was, "Do unto others as you would have them do unto you," and I erased religion from my conscious thought. However, there always remained a vague subconscious sense of void.

As I approached the age of 60, my employment had taken us to Austin, TX. At my wife's urging, we joined the First

Unitarian Universalist Church. The minister, Davidson Loehr, was a Biblical scholar, educated at the University of Chicago, and a member of Jesus Seminar. He not only introduced me to the work of the Jesus Seminar (1), but to the concept of the three different aspects of Jesus, upon which this analysis is based. For the record, I will define the three faces of Jesus as follows:

1) The Theological Jesus – The religions **about** Jesus, as defined by the various Christian theologies.
2) The Historical Jesus – The physical Jesus, as defined by historical records and archaeology.
3) The Spiritual Jesus – The Religion **of** Jesus, as defined by his spiritual teaching.

Since my retirement in 2001, I have been developing a personal understanding of the "Historical Jesus" through subscription to the Jesus Seminar Newsletter, reading books, Internet (Google) research, watching TV documentaries about Jesus, and DVD lectures.

THE LOST TOMB

In November of 2008, I completed the reading of *The Jesus Dynasty* (James Tabor, Simon & Schuster, April 4, 2006, ISBN-978-0743287234) and was very impressed with the scope and readability of this work. It has greatly augmented and clarified my own understanding of the "Historical Jesus", his family and original followers. Of particular interest was the reference to a Discovery Channel documentary *The Lost Tomb of Jesus*, first broadcast in 2007. This is a highly controversial/religiously incorrect documentary that both the Israeli (Jewish) Government and the conservative Christian establishment are trying to suppress/refute. It therefore has only been aired once. I immediately ordered a copy of the DVD online. Briefly, during the excavation for an apartment complex between Jerusalem and Bethlehem in 1980, a family tomb was unearthed. The linguistic forms of the names/nicknames on the ossuaries correlated with the biblically identified extended family and Disciples of Jesus of Nazareth/Son of Joseph, with a probability of 99.997 percent (2). Unfortunately, the significance of this archeological find was not understood before one of the ossuaries was stolen. The genetic material was returned for burial in accordance with Jewish tradition. The ossuaries were contaminated by being placed in the Jerusalem ossuary warehouse. Basic forensic and DNA analysis of potentially the greatest archeological find of all time could have resolved some of history's most important mysteries. However, we now know beyond a reasonable doubt that:

- The physical remains of Jesus were interned in a family tomb, probably having been moved from the temporary tomb where he was placed after his crucifixion.
- The tomb also originally contained the remains of his brother James who was executed in 62 CE. He was the last known leader of the direct followers of Jesus in Jerusalem.

Also of interest is the chevron over circle that appears above the entrance to the tomb and the cruder chevron over dot symbols that have been found incised on contemporary "Early Christian" ossuaries including that of Simon bar Jonahs, who helped Jesus carry his cross.

FROM JESUS TO CHRIST

The most critical input to both the "Historical" and "Spiritual" Jesus stories is an analysis of "The Baptism of Jesus in the Gospel of Mark," an article on the Ebionites in the Fourth R (Westar Institute) Volume 18 Number 5 September – October 2005, where Sakari Hakkinen, a Lutheran pastor and Diocese officer with a PhD in Theology, cites this Biblical passage:

> *Jesus came from Nazareth in Galilee and was baptized in the Jordan by John. And just as he got up out of the water, he saw the skies torn open and the Spirit like a dove descending into him. There was also a voice from the skies: "You are my favored son - I fully approve of you.* (Mark 1:9-1 1)

Hakkinen then asserts:

> *"In contrast with later evangelists, Mark here uses the Greek preposition eis ("into") to describe the descent of the Spirit into Jesus, not upon him, like most translations have it. The possession of Jesus by the Spirit was an early view of Jesus' significance. He was seen as a prophet who acted in the power of the Spirit.*
>
> *Mark obviously believed that Jesus received the Spirit only at his baptism, not before. The Spirit in fact possesses him at the moment of his baptism and immediately afterwards takes him to the desert.*

Jesus then preaches, heals, and exorcizes in the power of the Spirit. His true identity is recognized only by those possessed by spirits. The Gospel of Mark thus represents possessionist Christology in its most typical form: Jesus was an ordinary man—not divine—before he was filled with the Spirit at his baptism. Both the authors of the Gospels of Matthew and Luke rejected this kind of Christology, as can be seen in their narratives of Jesus' baptism (in which the Spirit descends upon, not into, Jesus) and in their addition of the birth and childhood stories of Jesus. For them, Jesus was the divine Son of God already from his birth."

Mark is the earliest Gospel writer that overlaps (in time) the original followers of Jesus. Mark's Gospel begins with the Baptism of Jesus and, in its original form, ends with the empty temporary tomb. We must assume that any part of the story that he left out was either because:

He considered it unimportant and irrelevant to the readers understanding of the "Good News"; or

He was unaware of those details, possibly because they had not yet been created.

It is interesting to note God's quote, *"You are my favored son - I fully approve of you."* This would imply that God has other children. After all, we are all children of God. Here, he is selecting Jesus as the favored one and, as we will see later, literally giving him the "Keys to the Kingdom." They didn't have cars in those days.

THE HISTORICAL JESUS

Now that we know the beginning and end of Jesus the Christ, let's return to Jesus of Nazareth. Before presenting an analysis of the Historical Jesus, I would like to lay out two principals:

1. Gospel means "good news." The gospels are editorial commercials representing the author(s) perception of the new, evolving, fragmented religion that we know as Christianity. Gospels were targeted at the conversion of a particular demographic group such as: Jews, Gentiles, Pagans, Romans, Greeks, or Gnostics. While based on real people and events, Gospels are not historical chronologies and are primarily based on evolving theological traditions that were transmitted orally for many years before being written down.

2. My education in math and science and many years of experience in business management have led me to conclude that there is no such thing as a complicated solution. There are simple solutions, and there are the problems caused by previous complicated solutions.

The later Gospel writers asserted that Jesus was the actual Son of God through Immaculate Conception and a Virgin Birth. While anything is possible, this is very unlikely. The original Gospel (Mark) makes no reference to a "Divine Birth." Mark specifically describes the entry and possession of Jesus by the Divine Spirit at his baptism, at which point he becomes the "adopted Son of God." In the first three canonical Gospels, Jesus does not claim to be a God or the "Son of God" and often refers to himself as the "Son of Man." Only in the last canonical gospel of John does Jesus claim to be God/Son of God, completing the evolution from the teachings of Jesus to a religion about Jesus. The divinity of Jesus is most likely a device of the later Gospel authors to elevate Jesus above the gods/prophets/ leaders of the other beliefs, from which they wished to gain converts.

Jesus and his younger brother James were known by the formal suffix "Son of Joseph." They were entombed by relatives with "Jesus Son of Joseph" and "James Son of Joseph" inscribed on their ossuaries. It is not unreasonable to conclude that Joseph was probably their father. Jesus' youngest brother/Mary's last son was known by a nickname (Yose "Joses," a diminutive of "Joseph"). Without the formal "Son of" suffix, we have no clue who was his father. However, it is likely that Joseph was deceased by the time of Joses' birth since it was not customary to name a child after a living relative.

It is not really important as to exactly when Jesus was born. However, it is human nature to want to know. So, I offer the following analysis. We know, from historical/biblical records, that he was born between 8 and 4 BCE. On the website http://www.eclipse.net/~molnar/ concerning *The Star of Bethlehem: The Legacy of the Magi* by Michael R. Molnar and published by Rutgers University Press. (ISBN: 0-8135-2701-5), there is the following question and answer:

> *"What was the Star (of Bethlehem)?*
>
> *On April 17, 6 BC two years before King Herod died Jupiter emerged in the east as a morning star in the sign of the Jews, Aries the Ram. The account in Matthew refers twice to the Star being in the east with good reasons. When the royal star of Zeus, the planet Jupiter, was in the east this was the most powerful time to confer kingships. Furthermore, the Sun was in Aries where it is exalted. The Moon was in very close conjunction with Jupiter in Aries. Modern calculations suggest that this was close enough to be an occultation (eclipse). The Sun's glare would have hidden that event. Saturn was also present which meant that the three rulers of Aries' trine (Sun, Jupiter, and Saturn) were present in Aries. Saturn and Jupiter were said to be "attendants" on the rising Sun, another regal aspect for astrologers. By modern expectations this is trivial. For ancient stargazers this configuration was truly awesome." (p. 96-101)*

The month of April also coincides with the only time of year that shepherds would be tending their flocks at night (referred to in Luke 2:8) to protect the spring lambs from predators.

We really don't know where Jesus was born. However, it almost certainly was not Bethlehem. Again, Mark makes no reference as to the location of his birth. However, there are contemporary historical records to verify that there was no census conducted in Galilee/Jerusalem around the date of his birth. The nearest one was some 10 years later. In any case, residents were counted where they lived, so they could be found. The Romans did not want their subjects running around the country going to their place of birth, but rather to stay home and keep working to pay their taxes. The attribution of the birth to Bethlehem is apparently an attempt by the Gospel writers to align Jesus with Old Testament prophecies that the messiah is coming from the "House of David"/Bethlehem. Since Jesus was known as "Jesus of Nazareth," I will go with the simple solution that he was probably born in or around Nazareth.

There is great confusion as to the relationship and relative ages of Jesus' siblings, caused by a conflict in religious dogma and a lack of biblical facts. It's been stated that:

- At least one of Jesus' sisters was from a previous marriage of Joseph and was in attendance at his birth.
- A different mother named his sister Mary, since children were never named after a living relative.
- One or two of Jesus' brothers were older stepbrothers from Joseph's previous marriage.
- There is general (non-Catholic) agreement that at least two brothers were younger brothers from Mary (3).

This is not significant to the historical Jesus story. The only relevance is that they were among his original followers and that James took over their leadership upon Jesus' death. Both James' and a younger brother's (nicknamed Joses) ossuaries contribute to the identification of the previously discussed family tomb.

There is much speculation and debate about the so-called "lost Years of Jesus" between birth and the beginning of his Ministry. From the Gospel of Mark, we learned that the reason that they were lost was because they were not important. During this period, Jesus acquired the experience, skills, and religious education that would be necessary to fulfill his ultimate mission. This time was probably spent in or around Nazareth and the larger neighboring city of Sepphoris.

The period between Jesus' Baptism and Crucifixion is variously documented in the Gospels and need not be reviewed in order to conclude the outline of the "Historical" Jesus. Obviously, the divine possession at the Baptism profoundly affected the "Spiritual" Jesus.

THE SPIRITUAL JESUS

I now turn to a subject that I have only recently begun to consider. This will require a great deal of education and analysis to adequately address, therefore I will outline the preliminary structure that I have developed for future research and conclusions.

We will never know the exact Divine Revelation that was instilled in Jesus during his Baptism or the details of the Belief System that he evolved over the next 40 days (a long time) of communing with God in the wilderness. In order to understand the spirituality of Jesus, we must reconstruct these things from his teachings. Unfortunately, 2,000 years of transcription errors, poor translations, editorializing, misattributions, and outright fabrications (Fake good News) have seriously clouded the record of Jesus' spoken words. The fact that he deliberately tried to obscure the meaning of his parables and sayings also contributes greatly to this problem. Even grouping them by the Jesus Seminar's "color codes" doesn't significantly alleviate their apparent confusing and contradictory nature. The Jesus

Seminar used font colors to indicate the probability that particular biblical quotations content and wording originated with the "Historical Jesus." Quotations printed in red are most likely the spoken words of Jesus.

What we need is the decoder ring, the encryption key, and the parsing filter to understand the underlying philosophy and structure of Jesus' teaching. That key was found over the entry of "the Jesus Family Tomb" and scratched into contemporary ossuaries. The symbol of the early followers of Jesus is known as "The Eye of God." After all, the use of a cross as a symbol then would be equivalent to the use of the electric chair today. The eye of God (4) is based on the specific eye of a specific god (Horus/Ra) of Egyptian mythology. However, in general usage it represents the "The Omni Presence of God".

The most relevant teaching of Jesus is that the Kingdom of God is not some faraway place in a faraway time that we can only dream about. It is here and now, among and within us. Jesus put it this way:

> *One day the Pharisees asked Jesus, "When will the Kingdom of God begin?" Jesus replied, "The Kingdom of God isn't ushered in with visible signs. You won't be able to say, 'It has begun here in this place or there in that part of the country. For the Kingdom of God is within you.'"* (TLB, Luke 17:20-21)

This is probably close to the spiritual inspiration that Jesus received from God.

The Gospel of Thomas (5) clearly and directly presents Jesus' teaching on the "Kingdom of God." Here Jesus says,

*If those who lead you say to you, "look, the Kingdom
is in the sky," then the birds will get there first. If
they say "it's in the ocean," then the fish will get there
first. But the Kingdom of God is within you and outside of you. Once you come to know yourselves, you
will become known. And you will know that it is you
who are the children of the living father. But if you
do not know yourselves, then you live in poverty, and
you are the poverty.* (Thomas 3)

Given that "The Kingdom of God is within you," the question
becomes how do we develop our divine spark, soul, or spiritual
existence as opposed to our natural self/mind generated ego-
centric reality?

*If you bring forth what is within you, what you
bring forth will save you. If you do not bring forth
what is within you, what you do not bring forth will
destroy you. (Thomas 70)*

Jesus, just as university professors do today, taught curricula ap-
propriate to student's level of intellectual development. The
"achieving the Kingdom of God on Earth" concept presented
in Thomas is a "Graduate Level" extension of the basic "works"
and/or "grace" as the dichotomy found in the canonical gospels.

Jesus addresses the Disciples: "'¹And he said to them, 'I tell
you the truth, some who are standing here will not taste death
before they see the kingdom of God come with power.'"
(Mark 9:1.)

Here Jesus is clearly referring to the few that will be able
to unlock the Kingdom of God that is within them.

The concept of "The Kingdom of God/Personal Spiritual Development" clarifies many of Jesus' Teachings, including:

- The disciples were amazed at his words. But Jesus said again, "Children, how hard it is to enter the kingdom of God! It is easier for a camel to go through the eye of a needle than for a rich man to enter the kingdom of God." (Mark 10:24-25)
- "Why do you look at the speck of sawdust in your brother's eye and pay no attention to the plank in your own eye? How can you say to your brother, 'Let me take the speck out of your eye,' when all the time there is a plank in your own eye?[5] You hypocrite, first take the plank out of your own eye, and then you will see clearly to remove the speck from your brother's eye." (Matthew 7:3-5)
- "He said to them, 'Do you bring in a lamp to put it under a bowl or a bed? Instead, don't you put it on its stand? For whatever is hidden is meant to be disclosed, and whatever is concealed is meant to be brought out into the open. If anyone has ears to hear, let him hear.' 'Consider carefully what you hear,' he continued. 'With the measure you use, it will be measured to you—and even more. Whoever has will be given more; whoever does not have, even what he has will be taken from him.'" (Mark 4:21-25)
- "But when you are invited, take the lowest place, so that when your host comes, he will say to you, 'Friend, move up to a better place.' Then you will be honored in the presence of all your fellow guests. For everyone who exalts himself will be humbled, and he who humbles himself will be exalted." (Luke 14:10-11)

- The disciples said to Jesus, "Tell us what Heaven's kingdom is like." He said to them, "It's like a mustard seed, the smallest of all seeds, but when it falls on prepared soil, it produces a large plant and becomes a shelter for birds of the sky." (Thomas 20)
- Jesus said, "Whoever drinks from my mouth will become like me; I myself shall become that person, and the hidden things will be revealed to him." (Thomas 108)
- His disciples said to him, "When will the kingdom come?" "It will not come by watching for it. It will not be said, 'Look, here!' or 'Look, there!' Rather, the Father's kingdom is spread out upon the earth, and people don't see it." (Thomas 113)
- *The Lord's Prayer* (Matthew 6:9-13; English vernacular version)

  Our Father who art in heaven,
  hallowed be thy name.
  Thy kingdom come.
  Thy will be done
  on **earth** as it is in heaven.
  Give us this day our daily bread,
  and forgive us our trespasses,
  as we forgive those who trespass against us,
  and lead us not into temptation,
  but deliver us from evil.
  For thine is the kingdom,
  and the power, and the glory,
  for ever and ever.
  Amen.

Conclusion

The Good News According to This Paul

The "Historical Jesus"

The preponderance of evidence indicates that Jesus of Nazareth:

- Was born a human child ~ April 17, 6 BCE in or around Nazareth.
- Matured from a precious adolescent into a relatively well-educated man.
- Was baptized by his cousin John the baptizer.
- Was immediately spiritually possessed by God
- Preached this spiritual reality for a short period of time.
- Died on the cross in Jerusalem.
- His physical remains were interned in a family tomb.

This "Historical Jesus" is completely compatible with all other monotheistic religions and, if not unifying, is at least harmonizing. They are all talking about the same God and only differ in teachers, philosophers and prophets. To paraphrase Rodney King, "Can't we all just get along"?

Whether through birth or baptism, Jesus of Nazareth was clearly selected by God to be the Messiah, the Christ, meaning the anointed one, to proclaim God's spiritual message on Earth.

The "Spiritual Jesus"

The Religion **of** Jesus is a philosophy based on the "Kingdom of God is in you" – which drives personal spiritual development. This concept represents the advanced spiritual teaching of Jesus, which was understood by only some of his Disciples, including his brother James, Judas, and Mary Magdalene as indicated in the "Gospel of Mary" (6). This connection between God and human spirituality is universally applicable and holds the potential of uniting Mankind. The Religion of Jesus is at once very powerful and very demanding. It requires every individual to develop their internal life force in order to realize the "Kingdom of God" on Earth.

Notes/References

(See Wikipedia, the free encyclopedia –
http://en.wikipedia.org/wiki/Main_Page)

1. The Jesus Seminar was a group of about 150 individuals, including scholars with advanced degrees in biblical studies, religious studies or related fields as well as published authors who are notable in the field of religion, founded in 1985 by the late Robert Funk and John Dominic Crossan under the auspices of the Westar Institute. One of the most active groups in biblical criticism, the seminar uses votes with colored beads to decide their collective view of the historicity of Jesus, specifically what he may or may not have said and done as a historical figure. In addition, the seminar popularizes the quest for the historical Jesus. The public was welcome to attend the twice-yearly meetings. They produced new translations of the New Testament and apocrypha to use as textual sources. They published their

results in three reports *The Five Gospels* (1993), *The Acts of Jesus* (1998), and *The Gospel of Jesus* (1999). They also ran a series of lectures and workshops in various U.S. cities.

2. Ossuary inscriptions associated with the "Jesus Family Tomb" – Six of the remaining nine, from the original 10, ossuaries have inscriptions. The other three ossuaries have no inscriptions. As translated in *The Lost Tomb of Jesus* and *The Jesus Family Tomb*, they read as follows:

*   *Yeshua bar Yehosef*, Aramaic for "Jesus son of Joseph"
*   *Maria*, written in Aramaic script, but a Latin form of the Hebrew name "Miriam" ("Mary")
*   *Yose*, a diminutive of "Joseph" mentioned (in its Greek form "Joses") as the name of one of Jesus's brothers in the New Testament (Mark 6:3)
*   *Yehuda bar Yeshua*, Possibly Aramaic for "Judah son of Jesus"
*   *Mariamene e Mara*. According to the filmmakers, this is Greek for "Mary known as the master." The similar name "Mariamne" is found in the Acts of Philip: Francois Bovon, professor of the history of religion at Harvard University has suggested based on his study of that work that Mariamene, or Mariamne, was the actual name of Mary Magdalene.
*   *Matya*, Hebrew for 'Matthew'—*not* claimed to be Matthew the Evangelist but "possibly a male relative of Mary or the husband of one of the women in an unmarked ossuary". The filmmakers claim that there is evidence that Mary mother of Jesus had many relatives named Matthew. Genealogists have purportedly traced

Mary's lineage back to the Priestly branch of the House of David in which Matthew is a common name.

The film further claims that the tenth ossuary, which went missing years ago, is the James Ossuary purported to contain the body of James, the brother of Jesus.

The execution of James – 62 CE

- Mass spectrograph testing proved that there was a match between the patina on the James and Yeshua` ossuaries and referred to the James ossuary as the "missing link" from the tomb of Yeshua` (Jesus);
- The ossuary that became missing from the tomb of Yeshua` had actually been the infamous James ossuary believed to contain the remains of the brother of Yeshua`. The ossuary was inscribed with "James son of Joseph" and the thieves apparently added the forged "Brother of Jesus". Since removed from the context of

the Jesus tomb, the original inscription would have no meaning/value.

The chance that a Jesus son of Joseph buried with four other people whose linguistic form and combination of six names that are clearly identified in the Bible as relatives/companion, is not the Jesus of Nazareth, is less than 1 in 30,000. This mathematically equates to a 99.997 percent certainty that the tomb contained Jesus' physical remains.

It is tempting to speculate that the child's ossuary inscribed "*Yehuda bar Yeshua*" or "Judah son of Jesus" belongs to the son of Jesus of Nazareth and Mary Magdalene. However, Jesus was a common name, and the tomb contained the marked and unmarked ossuaries of several women, anyone of which could have conceived a child with a different Jesus. The only way to confirm paternity is through nuclear DNA testing. The documentary indicated that the deteriorated genetic residue could only support mitochondrial testing for the determination of a maternal relationship. In any case, the remains are of a child and there is no evidence of any other offspring that could have potentially perpetuated the bloodline of Jesus.

3. Mary Mother of Jesus - Early traditions, first visible in the writings of Papias (during the first half of the 2nd century), have identified her sons James and Joses/Joseph with the "brothers of Jesus" of the same name and made her the mother of the "brethren of the Lord." This is the exact cluster of family names associated with the "Jesus Tomb," which strengthens the credibility of both hypotheses.

Mary of Clopas or Cleophas (Greek: *Maria he tou Klopa*), the wife of Clopas who is believed to be the brother of Joseph, was one of various Mary's named in the New Testament. Mary of Clopas is explicitly mentioned only in (John 19:25), where she is among the women present at the Crucifixion:

"Now there stood by the cross of Jesus His mother, and His mother's sister, Mary [the wife] of Clopas, and Mary Magdalene."

1st century Jewish tradition was for an unmarried brother to marry the widow of his deceased sibling. This has led some modern writers, such as Robert Eisenman and James Tabor, to claim that Mary of Clopas actually refers to Jesus' mother as well. It is possible that the youngest brother of Jesus (Joses) is the son of Clopas and Mary and was named after his deceased uncle Joseph. However, Mary of Clopas could just as likely refer to Mary's sister-in-law.

4. The Eye of Horus (Wedjat) (previously *Wadjet* and the Eye of the Moon; and afterwards as The Eye of Ra)[2] or ("Udjat") is an ancient Egyptian symbol of protection and royal power from deities Horus or Ra. The symbol is seen on images of Horus' mother, Isis, and on other deities associated with her. In the Egyptian language, the word for this symbol was "Wedjat." It was the eye of one of the earliest of Egyptian deities, Wadjet, who later became associated with Bast, Mut, and Hathor as well. Wedjat was a solar deity and this symbol began as her eye, an all-seeing eye.

The Definition and Meaning of the Eye as a Christian Symbol may be found at http://www.catholic-saints.info/ catholic-symbols/eye-christian-symbol.htm. The Eye Christian Symbol stands for the "all-seeing eye" representing the eye of God the Father, the all-knowing and ever-present God. In later examples of Christian art, the eye was pictured in a triangle with rays of light to represent the infinite holiness of the Trinity. The all Seeing Eye is based on the following passage in Psalm 33:18:

"But the eyes of the LORD are on those who fear him, on those whose hope is in his unfailing love."

5. The Gospel of Thomas (A Coptic papyrus manuscript discovered in 1945 at Nag Hammadi, Egypt.) begins, "These are the secret sayings that the living Jesus spoke and which Didymos Judas Thomas recorded." Both the words "Didymos" (Greek) and "Thomas" (Hebrew) mean "Twin" and are not actuall names. The teaching of salvation (i.e., entering the Kingdom of Heaven) that is found in The

Gospel of Thomas is neither that of "works" nor of "grace" as the dichotomy is found in the canonical gospels, but what might be called a third way, that of insight. The overriding concern of The Gospel of Thomas is to find the light within in order to be a light unto the world.

The PBS Font Line program "The Gospel of Thomas" offers the viewer his "secret teachings" about the Kingdom of God (http://www.pbs.org/wgbh/pages/frontline/shows/religion/story/thomas.html). Elaine H. Pagels, The Harrington Spear Paine Foundation Professor of Religion at Princeton University, states: "Now, [in the Gospel of Thomas], this Jesus comes to reveal that you and he are, if you like, twins... And what you discover as you read the Gospel of Thomas, which you're meant to discover, is that you and Jesus at a deep level are identical twins. And that you discover that you are the child of God just as he is. And so that at the end of the gospel Jesus speaks to Thomas and says, 'Whoever drinks from my mouth will become as I am, and I will become that person, and the mysteries will be revealed to him.'"

The Gospel of Thomas does not refer to Jesus as "Christ," "Lord," or "Son of Man" as the New Testament does, but simply as "Jesus." Since the Gospel of Thomas is a "Sayings Gospel," it also lacks any mention of Jesus' birth, baptism, miracles, travels, death, and resurrection. However, over half of the sayings in Thomas are similar to sayings and parables found in the canonical gospels.

THE TEXT OF THE GOSPEL OF THOMAS

These are the secret sayings which the living Jesus spoke and which Didymos Judas Thomas wrote down.

(1) And he said, "Whoever finds the interpretation of these sayings will not experience death."

(2) Jesus said, "Let him who seeks continue seeking until he finds. When he finds, he will become troubled. When he becomes troubled, he will be astonished, and he will rule over the All."

(3) Jesus said, "If those who lead you say to you, 'See, the kingdom is in the sky,' then the birds of the sky will precede you. If they say to you, 'It is in the sea,' then the fish will precede you. Rather, the kingdom is inside of you, and it is outside of you. When you come to know yourselves, then you will become known, and you will realize that it is you who are the sons of

the living father. But if you will not know yourselves, you dwell in poverty and it is you who are that poverty."

(4) Jesus said, "The man old in days will not hesitate to ask a small child seven days old about the place of life, and he will live. For many who are first will become last, and they will become one and the same."

(5) Jesus said, "Recognize what is in your sight, and that which is hidden from you will become plain to you. For there is nothing hidden which will not become manifest."

(6) His disciples questioned him and said to him, "Do you want us to fast? How shall we pray? Shall we give alms? What diet shall we observe?"

Jesus said, "Do not tell lies, and do not do what you hate, for all things are plain in the sight of heaven. For nothing hidden will not become manifest, and nothing covered will remain without being uncovered."

(7) Jesus said, "Blessed is the lion which becomes man when consumed by man; and cursed is the man whom the lion consumes, and the lion becomes man."

(8) And he said, "The man is like a wise fisherman who cast his net into the sea and drew it up from the sea full of small fish. Among them the wise fisherman found a fine large fish. He threw all the small fish back into the sea and chose the large fish without difficulty. Whoever has ears to hear, let him hear."

(9) Jesus said, "Now the sower went out, took a handful (of seeds), and scattered them. Some fell on the road; the birds came and gathered them up. Others fell on the rock, did not take root in the soil, and did not produce ears. And others fell on thorns; they choked the seed(s) and worms ate them. And others fell on the good soil and it produced good fruit: it bore sixty per measure and a hundred and twenty per measure."

(10) Jesus said, "I have cast fire upon the world, and see, I am guarding it until it blazes."

(11) Jesus said, "This heaven will pass away, and the one above it will pass away. The dead are not alive, and the living will not die. In the days when you consumed what is dead, you made it what is alive. When you come to dwell in the light, what will you do? On the day when you were one you became two. But when you become two, what will you do?"

(12) The disciples said to Jesus, "We know that you will depart from us. Who is to be our leader?"

Jesus said to them, "Wherever you are, you are to go to James the righteous, for whose sake heaven and earth came into being."

(13) Jesus said to his disciples, "Compare me to someone and tell me whom I am like."

Simon Peter said to him, "You are like a righteous angel."

Matthew said to him, "You are like a wise philosopher."

Thomas said to him, "Master, my mouth is wholly incapable of saying whom you are like."

Jesus said, "I am not your master. Because you have drunk, you have become intoxicated from the bubbling spring which I have measured out."

And he took him and withdrew and told him three things. When Thomas returned to his companions, they asked him, "What did Jesus say to you?"

Thomas said to them, "If I tell you one of the things which he told me, you will pick up stones and throw them at me; a fire will come out of the stones and burn you up."

(14) Jesus said to them, "If you fast, you will give rise to sin for yourselves; and if you pray, you will be condemned; and if you give alms, you will do harm to your spirits. When you go into any land and walk about in the districts, if they receive you, eat what they will set before you, and heal the sick among them. For what goes into your mouth will not defile you, but that which issues from your mouth - it is that which will defile you."

(15) Jesus said, "When you see one who was not born of woman, prostrate yourselves on your faces and worship him. That one is your father."

(16) Jesus said, "Men think, perhaps, that it is peace which I have come to cast upon the world. They do not know that it is dissension which I have come to cast upon the earth: fire, sword, and war. For there will be five in a house: three will be against two, and two against three, the father against the son, and the son against the father. And they will stand solitary."

(17) Jesus said, "I shall give you what no eye has seen and what no ear has heard and what no hand has touched and what has never occurred to the human mind."

(18) The disciples said to Jesus, "Tell us how our end will be."

Jesus said, "Have you discovered, then, the beginning, that you look for the end? For where the beginning is, there will the end be. Blessed is he who will take his place in the beginning; he will know the end and will not experience death."

(19) Jesus said, "Blessed is he who came into being before he came into being. If you become my disciples and listen to my words, these stones will minister to you. For there are five trees for you in Paradise which remain undisturbed summer and winter and whose leaves do not fall. Whoever becomes acquainted with them will not experience death."

(20) The disciples said to Jesus, "Tell us what the kingdom of heaven is like."

He said to them, "It is like a mustard seed. It is the smallest of all seeds. But when it falls on tilled soil, it produces a great plant and becomes a shelter for birds of the sky."

(21) Mary said to Jesus, "Whom are your disciples like?"

He said, "They are like children who have settled in a field which is not theirs. When the owners of the field come, they will say, 'Let us have back our field.' They (will) undress in their presence in order to let them have back their field and to give it back to them. Therefore I say, if the owner of a house knows that the thief is coming, he will begin his vigil before he comes and will not let him dig through into his house of his domain to carry away his goods. You, then, be on your guard against the world.

Arm yourselves with great strength lest the robbers find a way to come to you, for the difficulty which you expect will (surely) materialize. Let there be among you a man of understanding.

When the grain ripened, he came quickly with his sickle in his hand and reaped it. Whoever has ears to hear, let him hear."

(22) Jesus saw infants being suckled. He said to his disciples, "These infants being suckled are like those who enter the kingdom."

They said to him, "Shall we then, as children, enter the kingdom?"

Jesus said to them, "When you make the two one, and when you make the inside like the outside and the outside like the inside, and the above like the below, and when you make the male and the female one and the same, so that the male not be male nor the female; and when you fashion eyes in the place of an eye, and a hand in place of a hand, and a foot in place of a foot, and a likeness in place of a likeness; then will you enter the kingdom."

(23) Jesus said, "I shall choose you, one out of a thousand, and two out of ten thousand, and they shall stand as a single one."

(24) His disciples said to him, "Show us the place where you are, since it is necessary for us to seek it."

He said to them, "Whoever has ears, let him hear. There is light within a man of light, and he lights up the whole world. If he does not shine, he is darkness."

(25) Jesus said, "Love your brother like your soul, guard him like the pupil of your eye."

(26) Jesus said, "You see the mote in your brother's eye, but you do not see the beam in your own eye. When you cast the beam out of your own eye, then you will see clearly to cast the mote from your brother's eye."

(27) <Jesus said,> "If you do not fast as regards the world, you will not find the kingdom. If you do not observe the Sabbath as a Sabbath, you will not see the father."

(28) Jesus said, "I took my place in the midst of the world, and I appeared to them in flesh. I found all of them intoxicated; I found none of them thirsty. And my soul became afflicted for the sons of men, because they are blind in their hearts and do not have sight; for empty they came into the world, and empty too they seek to leave the world. But for the moment they are intoxicated. When they shake off their wine, then they will repent."

(29) Jesus said, "If the flesh came into being because of spirit, it is a wonder. But if spirit came into being because of the body, it is a wonder of wonders. Indeed, I am amazed at how this great wealth has made its home in this poverty."

(30) Jesus said, "Where there are three gods, they are gods. Where there are two or one, I am with him."

(31) Jesus said, "No prophet is accepted in his own village; no physician heals those who know him."

(32) Jesus said, "A city being built on a high mountain and fortified cannot fall, nor can it be hidden."

(33) Jesus said, "Preach from your housetops that which you will hear in your ear. For no one lights a lamp and puts it under a bushel, nor does he put it in a hidden place, but rather he sets it on a lamp stand so that everyone who enters and leaves will see its light."

(34) Jesus said, "If a blind man leads a blind man, they will both fall into a pit."

(35) Jesus said, "It is not possible for anyone to enter the house of a strong man and take it by force unless he binds his hands; then he will (be able to) ransack his house."

(36) Jesus said, "Do not be concerned from morning until evening and from evening until morning about what you will wear."

(37) His disciples said, "When will you become revealed to us and when shall we see you?"

Jesus said, "When you disrobe without being ashamed and take up your garments and place them under your feet like little children and tread on them, then will you see the son of the living one, and you will not be afraid"

(38) Jesus said, "Many times have you desired to hear these words which I am saying to you, and you have no one else to hear them from. There will be days when you will look for me and will not find me."

(39) Jesus said, "The pharisees and the scribes have taken the keys of knowledge (gnosis) and hidden them. They themselves have not entered, nor have they allowed to enter those who wish to. You, however, be as wise as serpents and as innocent as doves."

(40) Jesus said, "A grapevine has been planted outside of the father, but being unsound, it will be pulled up by its roots and destroyed."

(41) Jesus said, "Whoever has something in his hand will receive more, and whoever has nothing will be deprived of even the little he has."

(42) Jesus said, "Become passers-by."

(43) His disciples said to him, "Who are you, that you should say these things to us?" <Jesus said to them,> "You do not realize who I am from what I say to you, but you have become like the Jews, for they (either) love the tree and hate its fruit (or) love the fruit and hate the tree."

(44) Jesus said, "Whoever blasphemes against the father will be forgiven, and whoever blasphemes against the son will be forgiven, but whoever blasphemes against the holy spirit will not be forgiven either on earth or in heaven."

(45) Jesus said, "Grapes are not harvested from thorns, nor are figs gathered from thistles, for they do not produce fruit. A good man brings forth good from his storehouse; an evil man brings forth evil things from his evil storehouse, which is in his heart, and says evil things. For out of the abundance of the heart he brings forth evil things."

(46) Jesus said, "Among those born of women, from Adam until John the Baptist, there is no one so superior to John the Baptist that his eyes should not be lowered (before him). Yet

I have said, whichever one of you comes to be a child will be acquainted with the kingdom and will become superior to John."

(47) Jesus said, "It is impossible for a man to mount two horses or to stretch two bows. And it is impossible for a servant to serve two masters; otherwise, he will honor the one and treat the other contemptuously. No man drinks old wine and immediately desires to drink new wine. And new wine is not put into old wineskins, lest they burst; nor is old wine put into a new wineskin, lest it spoil it. An old patch is not sewn onto a new garment, because a tear would result."

(48) Jesus said, "If two make peace with each other in this one house, they will say to the mountain, 'Move Away,' and it will move away."

(49) Jesus said, "Blessed are the solitary and elect, for you will find the kingdom. For you are from it, and to it you will return."

(50) Jesus said, "If they say to you, 'Where did you come from?', say to them, 'We came from the light, the place where the light came into being on its own accord and established itself and became manifest through their image.' If they say to you, 'Is it you?', say, 'We are its children, we are the elect of the living father.' If they ask you, 'What is the sign of your father in you?', say to them, 'It is movement and repose.'"

(51) His disciples said to him, "When will the repose of the dead come about, and when will the new world come?"

He said to them, "What you look forward to has already come, but you do not recognize it."

(52) His disciples said to him, "Twenty-four prophets spoke in Israel, and all of them spoke in you."

He said to them, "You have omitted the one living in your presence and have spoken (only) of the dead."

(53) His disciples said to him, "Is circumcision beneficial or not?"

He said to them, "If it were beneficial, their father would beget them already circumcised from their mother. Rather, the true circumcision in spirit has become completely profitable."

(54) Jesus said, "Blessed are the poor, for yours is the kingdom of heaven."

(55) Jesus said, "Whoever does not hate his father and his mother cannot become a discile to me. And whoever does not hate his brothers and sisters and take up his cross in my way will not be worthy of me."

(56) Jesus said, "Whoever has come to understand the world has found (only) a corpse, and whoever has found a corpse is superior to the world."

(57) Jesus said, "The kingdom of the father is like a man who had good seed. His enemy came by night and sowed weeds among the good seed. The man did not allow them to pull up the weeds; he said to them, 'I am afraid that you will go intending to pull up the weeds and pull up the wheat along with them.' For on the day of the harvest the weeds will be plainly visible, and they will be pulled up and burned."

(58) Jesus said, "Blessed is the man who has suffered and found life."

(59) Jesus said, "Take heed of the living one while you are alive, lest you die and seek to see him and be unable to do so."

(60) <They saw> a Samaritan carrying a lamb on his way to Judea. He said to his disciples, "That man is round about the lamb." They said to him, "So that he may kill it and eat it."

He said to them, "While it is alive, he will not eat it, but only when he has killed it and it has become a corpse."

They said to him, "He cannot do so otherwise."

He said to them, "You too, look for a place for yourself within repose, lest you become a corpse and be eaten."

(61) Jesus said, "Two will rest on a bed: the one will die, and the other will live." Salome said, "Who are you, man, that you ... have come up on my couch and eaten from my table?"

Jesus said to her, "I am he who exists from the undivided. I was given some of the things of my father."

<...> "I am your disciple."

<...> "Therefore I say, if he is destroyed, he will be filled with light, but if he is divided, he will be filled with darkness."

(62) Jesus said, "It is to those who are worthy of my mysteries that I tell my mysteries. Do not let your left (hand) know what your right (hand) is doing."

(63) Jesus said, "There was a rich man who had much money. He said, 'I shall put my money to use so that I may sow, reap, plant, and fill my storehouse with produce, with the result that

I shall lack nothing.' Such were his intentions, but that same night he died. Let him who has ears hear."

(64) Jesus said, "A man had received visitors. And when he had prepared the dinner, he sent his servant to invite the guests.

He went to the first one and said to him, 'My master invites you.' He said, 'I have claims against some merchants. They are coming to me this evening. I must go and give them my orders. I ask to be excused from the dinner.'

He went to another and said to him, 'My master has invited you.' He said to him, 'I have just bought a house and am required for the day. I shall not have any spare time.' He went to another and said to him, 'My master invites you.' He said to him, 'My friend is going to get married, and I am to prepare the banquet. I shall not be able to come. I ask to be excused from the dinner.'

He went to another and said to him, 'My master invites you.' He said, 'I have just bought a farm, and I am on my way to collect the rent. I shall not be able to come. I ask to be excused.'

The servant returned and said to his master, 'Those whom you invited to the dinner have asked to be excused.' The master said to his servant, 'Go outside to the streets and bring back those whom you happen to meet, so that they may dine.' Businessmen and merchants will not enter the places of my father."

(65) He said, "There was a good man who owned a vineyard. He leased it to tenant farmers so that they might work it and he might collect the produce from them. He sent his servant so that the tenants might give him the produce of the vineyard. They seized his servant and beat him, all but killing him. The

servant went back and told his master. The master said, 'Perhaps he did not recognize them.' He sent another servant. The tenants beat this one as well. Then the owner sent his son and said, 'Perhaps they will show respect to my son.' Because the tenants knew that it was he who was the heir to the vineyard, they seized him and killed him. Let him who has ears hear."

(66) Jesus said, "Show me the stone which the builders have rejected. That one is the cornerstone."

(67) Jesus said, "If one who knows the all still feels a personal deficiency, he is completely deficient."

(68) Jesus said, "Blessed are you when you are hated and persecuted. Wherever you have been persecuted they will find no place."

(69) Jesus said, "Blessed are they who have been persecuted within themselves. It is they who have truly come to know the father. Blessed are the hungry, for the belly of him who desires will be filled."

(70) Jesus said, "That which you have will save you if you bring it forth from yourselves. That which you do not have within you will kill you if you do not have it within you."

(71) Jesus said, "I shall destroy this house, and no one will be able to build it [...]."

(72) A man said to him, "Tell my brothers to divide my father's possessions with me."

He said to him, "O man, who has made me a divider?"

He turned to his disciples and said to them, "I am not a divider, am I?"

(73) Jesus said, "The harvest is great but the laborers are few. Beseech the Lord, therefore, to send out laborers to the harvest."

(74) He said, "O Lord, there are many around the drinking trough, but there is nothing in the cistern."

(75) Jesus said, "Many are standing at the door, but it is the solitary who will enter the bridal chamber."

(76) Jesus said, "The kingdom of the father is like a merchant who had a consignment of merchandise and who discovered a pearl. That merchant was shrewd. He sold the merchandise and bought the pearl alone for himself. You too, seek his unfailing and enduring treasure where no moth comes near to devour and no worm destroys."

(77) Jesus said, "It is I who am the light which is above them all. It is I who am the all. From me did the all come forth, and unto me did the all extend. Split a piece of wood, and I am there. Lift up the stone, and you will find me there."

(78) Jesus said, "Why have you come out into the desert? To see a reed shaken by the wind? And to see a man clothed in fine garments like your kings and your great men? Upon them are the fine garments, and they are unable to discern the truth."

(79) A woman from the crowd said to him, "Blessed are the womb which bore you and the breasts which nourished you."

He said to her, "Blessed are those who have heard the word of the father and have truly kept it. For there will be days when you will say, 'Blessed are the womb which has not conceived and the breasts which have not given milk.'"

(80) Jesus said, "He who has recognized the world has found the body, but he who has found the body is superior to the world."

(81) Jesus said, "Let him who has grown rich be king, and let him who possesses power renounce it."

(82) Jesus said, "He who is near me is near the fire, and he who is far from me is far from the kingdom."

(83) Jesus said, "The images are manifest to man, but the light in them remains concealed in the image of the light of the father. He will become manifest, but his image will remain concealed by his light."

(84) Jesus said, "When you see your likeness, you rejoice. But when you see your images which came into being before you, and which neither die not become manifest, how much you will have to bear!"

(85) Jesus said, "Adam came into being from a great power and a great wealth, but he did not become worthy of you. For had he been worthy, he would not have experienced death."

(86) Jesus said, "The foxes have their holes and the birds have their nests, but the son of man has no place to lay his head and rest."

(87) Jesus said, "Wretched is the body that is dependant upon a body, and wretched is the soul that is dependent on these two." (88) Jesus said, "The angels and the prophets will come to you and give to you those things you (already) have. And you too, give them those things which you have, and say to yourselves, 'When will they come and take what is theirs?'"

(89) Jesus said, "Why do you wash the outside of the cup? Do you not realize that he who made the inside is the same one who made the outside?"

(90) Jesus said, "Come unto me, for my yoke is easy and my lordship is mild, and you will find repose for yourselves."

(91) They said to him, "Tell us who you are so that we may believe in you." He said to them, "You read the face of the sky and of the earth, but you have not recognized the one who is before you, and you do not know how to read this moment."

(92) Jesus said, "Seek and you will find. Yet, what you asked me about in former times and which I did not tell you then, now I do desire to tell, but you do not inquire after it."

(93) <Jesus said,> "Do not give what is holy to dogs, lest they throw them on the dungheap. Do not throw the pearls to swine, lest they [...] it [...]."

(94) Jesus said, "He who seeks will find, and he who knocks will be let in."

(95) Jesus said, "If you have money, do not lend it at interest, but give it to one from whom you will not get it back."

(96) Jesus said, "The kingdom of the father is like a certain woman. She took a little leaven, concealed it in some dough, and made it into large loaves. Let him who has ears hear."

(97) Jesus said, "The kingdom of the father is like a certain woman who was carrying a jar full of meal. While she was walking on the road, still some distance from home, the handle of the jar broke and the meal emptied out behind her on the road. She did not realize it; she had noticed no accident. When she reached her house, she set the jar down and found it empty."

(98) Jesus said, "The kingdom of the father is like a certain man who wanted to kill a powerful man. In his own house he drew his sword and stuck it into the wall in order to find out whether his hand could carry through. Then he slew the powerful man."

(99) The disciples said to him, "Your brothers and your mother are standing outside." He said to them, "Those here who do the will of my father are my brothers and my mother. It is they who will enter the kingdom of my father."

(100) They showed Jesus a gold coin and said to him, "Caesar's men demand taxes from us."

He said to them, "Give Caesar what belongs to Caesar, give God what belongs to God, and give me what is mine."

(101) <Jesus said,> "Whoever does not hate his father and his mother as I do cannot become a disciple to me. And whoever does not love his father and his mother as I do cannot become a disciple to me. For my mother [...], but my true mother gave me life."

(102) Jesus said, "Woe to the pharisees, for they are like a dog sleeping in the manger of oxen, for neither does he eat nor does he let the oxen eat."

(103) Jesus said, "Fortunate is the man who knows where the brigands will enter, so that he may get up, muster his domain, and arm himself before they invade."

(104) They said to Jesus, "Come, let us pray today and let us fast."
Jesus said, "What is the sin that I have committed, or wherein have I been defeated? But when the bridegroom leaves the bridal chamber, then let them fast and pray."

(105) Jesus said, "He who knows the father and the mother will be called the son of a harlot."

(106) Jesus said, "When you make the two one, you will become the sons of man, and when you say, 'Mountain, move away,' it will move away."

(107) Jesus said, "The kingdom is like a shepherd who had a hundred sheep. One of them, the largest, went astray. He left the ninety-nine sheep and looked for that one until he found it. When he had gone to such trouble, he said to the sheep, 'I care for you more than the ninety-nine.'"

(108) Jesus said, "He who will drink from my mouth will become like me. I myself shall become he, and the things that are hidden will be revealed to him."

(109) Jesus said, "The kingdom is like a man who had a hidden treasure in his field without knowing it. And after he died, he left it to his son. The son did not know (about the treasure). He inherited the field and sold it. And the one who bought it went plowing and found the treasure. He began to lend money at interest to whomever he wished."

(110) Jesus said, "Whoever finds the world and becomes rich, let him renounce the world."

(111) Jesus said, "The heavens and the earth will be rolled up in your presence. And the one who lives from the living one will not see death." Does not Jesus say, "Whoever finds himself is superior to the world?"

(112) Jesus said, "Woe to the flesh that depends on the soul; woe to the soul that depends on the flesh."

(113) His disciples said to him, "When will the kingdom come?"
    <Jesus said,> "It will not come by waiting for it. It will not be a matter of saying 'here it is' or 'there it is.' Rather, the kingdom of the father is spread out upon the earth, and men do not see it."
    [The following final saying was apparently fabricated at a later date and tacked on , to justify the exclusion of women from the Priesthood. Especially ironic, since the very first Priest(ess) was Mary Magdalene (see The Gospel of Mary below).]

(114) Simon Peter said to him, "Let Mary leave us, for women are not worthy of life." Jesus said, "I myself shall lead her in order to make her male, so that she too may become a living spirit resembling you males. For every woman who will make herself male will enter the kingdom of heaven."

The Gospel According to Thomas
Marquette University
https://www.marquette.edu/maqom/Gospel%20of%20Thomas%20Lambdin.pdf

THE GOSPEL ACCORDING TO MARY MAGDALENE
(The Gospel of Mary)

"The *Gospel of Mary* is found in the *Berlin Gnostic Codex* (*Papyrus Berolinensis 8502*). This very important and well-preserved codex was discovered in the late-nineteenth century somewhere near Akhmim in upper Egypt. It was purchased in Cairo in

1896 by a German scholar, Dr. Carl Reinhardt, and then taken to Berlin.

The codex (as these ancient books are called) was probably copied and bound in the late fourth or early fifth century. It contains Coptic translations of three very important early Christian Gnostic texts: the *Gospel of Mary*, the *Apocryphon of John*, and the *Sophia of Jesus Christ*. The texts themselves date to the second century and were originally authored in Greek." See http://www.gnosis.org/library/marygosp.htm **The Gnostic Society Library**

Chapter 4
(Pages 1 to 6 of the manuscript, containing chapters 1-3, are lost. The extant text starts on page 7…)
. . . Will matter then be destroyed or not?
22) The Savior said, All nature, all formations, all creatures exist in and with one another, and they will be resolved again into their own roots.
23) For the nature of matter is resolved into the roots of its own nature alone.
24) He who has ears to hear, let him hear.
25) Peter said to him, Since you have explained everything to us, tell us this also: What is the sin of the world?
26) The Savior said There is no sin, but it is you who make sin when you do the things that are like the nature of adultery, which is called sin.
27) That is why the Good came into your midst, to the essence of every nature in order to restore it to its root.
28) Then He continued and said, That is why you become sick and die, for you are deprived of the one who can heal you.

29) He who has a mind to understand, let him understand.

30) Matter gave birth to a passion that has no equal, which proceeded from something contrary to nature. Then there arises a disturbance in its whole body.

31) That is why I said to you, Be of good courage, and if you are discouraged be encouraged in the presence of the different forms of nature.

32) He who has ears to hear, let him hear.

33) When the Blessed One had said this, He greeted them all, saying, Peace be with you. Receive my peace unto yourselves.

34) Beware that no one lead you astray saying Lo here or lo there! For the Son of Man is within you.

35) Follow after Him!

36) Those who seek Him will find Him.

37) Go then and preach the gospel of the Kingdom.

38) Do not lay down any rules beyond what I appointed you, and do not give a law like the lawgiver lest you be constrained by it.

39) When He said this He departed.

Chapter 5

1) But they were grieved. They wept greatly, saying, How shall we go to the Gentiles and preach the gospel of the Kingdom of the Son of Man? If they did not spare Him, how will they spare us?

2) Then Mary stood up, greeted them all, and said to her brethren, Do not weep and do not grieve nor be irresolute, for His grace will be entirely with you and will protect you.

3) But rather, let us praise His greatness, for He has prepared us and made us into Men.

4) When Mary said this, she turned their hearts to the Good, and they began to discuss the words of the Savior.

5) Peter said to Mary, Sister we know that the Savior loved you more than the rest of woman.

6) Tell us the words of the Savior which you remember which you know, but we do not, nor have we heard them.

7) Mary answered and said, What is hidden from you I will proclaim to you.

8) And she began to speak to them these words: I, she said, I saw the Lord in a vision and I said to Him, Lord I saw you today in a vision. He answered and said to me,

9) Blessed are you that you did not waver at the sight of Me. For where the mind is there is the treasure.

10) I said to Him, Lord, how does he who sees the vision see it, through the soul or through the spirit?

11) The Savior answered and said, He does not see through the soul nor through the spirit, but the mind that is between the two that is what sees the vision and it is [...]

(pages 11-14 are missing from the manuscript)

Chapter 8:

. . . it.

10) And desire said, I did not see you descending, but now I see you ascending. Why do you lie since you belong to me?

11) The soul answered and said, I saw you. You did not see me nor recognize me. I served you as a garment and you did not know me.

12) When it said this, it (the soul) went away rejoicing greatly.

13) Again it came to the third power, which is called ignorance.

14) The power questioned the soul, saying, Where are you

going? In wickedness are you bound. But you are bound; do not judge!

15) And the soul said, Why do you judge me, although I have not judged?

16) I was bound, though I have not bound.

17) I was not recognized. But I have recognized that the All is being dissolved, both the earthly things and the heavenly.

18) When the soul had overcome the third power, it went upwards and saw the fourth power, which took seven forms.

19) The first form is darkness, the second desire, the third ignorance, the fourth is the excitement of death, the fifth is the kingdom of the flesh, the sixth is the foolish wisdom of flesh, the seventh is the wrathful wisdom. These are the seven powers of wrath.

20) They asked the soul, Whence do you come slayer of men, or where are you going, conqueror of space?

21) The soul answered and said, What binds me has been slain, and what turns me about has been overcome,

22) and my desire has been ended, and ignorance has died.

23) In an aeon I was released from a world, and in a Type from a type, and from the fetter of oblivion which is transient.

24) From this time on will I attain to the rest of the time, of the season, of the aeon, in silence.

Chapter 9

1) When Mary had said this, she fell silent, since it was to this point that the Savior had spoken with her.

2) But Andrew answered and said to the brethren, Say what you wish to say about what she has said. I at least do not believe that the Savior said this. For certainly these teachings are strange ideas.

3) Peter answered and spoke concerning these same things.
4) He questioned them about the Savior: Did He really speak privately with a woman and not openly to us? Are we to turn about and all listen to her? Did He prefer her to us?
5) Then Mary wept and said to Peter, My brother Peter, what do you think? Do you think that I have thought this up myself in my heart, or that I am lying about the Savior?
6) Levi answered and said to Peter, Peter you have always been hot tempered.
7) Now I see you contending against the woman like the adversaries.
8) But if the Savior made her worthy, who are you indeed to reject her? Surely the Savior knows her very well.
9) That is why He loved her more than us. Rather let us be ashamed and put on the perfect Man, and separate as He commanded us and preach the gospel, not laying down any other rule or other law beyond what the Savior said.
10) And when they heard this they began to go forth to proclaim and to preach.

The Gospel of Mary
The Gnostic Society
http://gnosis.org/library/marygosp.htm